WHY MOTO

Chris Keller

WHY MOTO

WHY MOTO

There are very few things in this world that we are unable to describe. Things that the human mind, body, and soul can only experience. I believe that somewhere between the spark, the fuel, and the air lies this moment. It is a moment that does not come at the start of the engine or at the end of the ride. This is a moment that anyone who has merged their being with the machine beneath them has felt. It is quiet, it is strength, it is peace, it is solace, it is happiness, it is moto.

The goal of this project is to connect the world through this feeling.

Why do you ride? Why do you wrench? Why do you moto? Why do you seek that feeling?

I have found that throughout my life I always come back to this moment, time and time again, and I know I am not alone. I want to share this moment, to share the reasons we seek it, the feelings it brings us, and how we can use it to unlock the world. It does not matter what kind of bike you ride, on what kind of terrain you ride it, or even if you find this moment simply at the turn of a wrench. We all feel it.

So whenever you are ready, in whatever form you wish, head to our social pages and tell us your story.

Website: www.whymoto.com
Instagram: @whydoyoumoto
X (formerly Twitter): @whydoyoumoto
Email: Whydoyoumoto@gmail.com

This book is for the wanderer, it is for the person that has never thought to swing a leg over a motorcycle, for the new, for the experienced. There is so much to be said about the motorcycle industry but often times not enough said about that moment right before one decides to join this family. What we hope to accomplish in this book is to give the reader the insight as to why, why we moto, and what this adventure can do for the human soul.

They say that you can't know the true feeling of an experience until you have lived it. That is true. Yet, I believe that experience dies if it is lived by one and not shared with others. As humans we all do it. We have that thing, that brings us peace.

The feeling that I get while riding, the feeling that I got as a young child, pedaling as fast as I could and then slamming my rear brake. The skid, the slide, the controlled out of control feeling that moved beneath me. It was my fingers, pulling a lever, tightening a cable down a line to a spring, the closing of a spring, the tightening of the brake pad against the wheel, the locking of the wheel, the friction of the tire on the asphalt, and the slide of that tire, that brought my freedom. This is what sets a ride apart. The search for the freedom from the decisions we have made in our life. Our lives are a series of decisions. Thoughts, actions, intentions, goals, desires, emotions all playing out with each new step, with each new conversation. When we are on our bikes or in our garage, it stops. The soul and the mind work as one, examining our road ahead, transporting our thoughts to a distant locker and we merge every sense with the world around us.

Freedom

We ride for freedom. That word throughout history has so many meanings to so many different generations, cultures, and races. Yet if you say this word in any language it invokes a spirit of undeniable peace and boundless limit. The freedom to be, to be who you once were, who you are now, or who you wish to become. Moto gives us this chance. Each of us lives inside a world that bears many definitions for freedom. Perhaps it is the ability to choose ones clothes, to choose ones family, to choose ones education, to choose our food, to choose our path. However, maybe it is none of those things. Moto provides, in our own unique worlds, the opportunity to shed those limits. Your ride may be days long, it may be hours long, or perhaps it is just minutes long. The beauty is the feeling does not change no matter the circumstance. The freedom that moto provides is one of simplicity and ease. Make your decisions, choose your path, twist your hand, and explore the sense of freedom.

Escape

Our lives are a simple series of choices. From the day we are born we make choices that impact the world around us and ripple throughout generations. Whether those choices bring joy, happiness, regret, frustration, or sadness, moto provides a brief moment of escape from it all. There is a point during a ride, one that is not planned or even thought into existence. It is after the nervousness of the cold motor has warmed, before we have decided to turn around and head back into our reality, it is a moment of silence. In that silence we find our escape.

Adventure

More, further, beyond the horizon. Adventure has lived within the human soul since the birth of mankind and lives on in our soul to this day. Embracing the thought of setting out in a direction and not knowing what lies ahead around that next turn. What obstacle will I have the opportunity to overcome? What technique will I be required to use? What awaits for me in the beyond? Moto provides us with a sense of adventure that defines the human spirit. Whether it is a long country road to nowhere, a dimly light forest trail, or a trip without a return date. Your adventure awaits at the turning of a motor.

Community

We are a community of one. When we are born into this world some are lucky enough to have a family and some are lucky enough to find a family, but no matter the circumstance, the shared human condition is a bond that threads the needle of our existence. Throughout our life we develop our identities. It is a sense of self that never fades but it can be overshadowed by experiences, outside opinions, and hardships. When we find our true form, we often find those who share our view on the world around us. There is hate, there is jealously there is anger, there is greed, there is evil. There is love, there is passion, there is trust, there is success. And then there is moto. The beautiful idea of this moto community is that nothing matters. It does not matter where you are from, what job you have to provide for yourself or your family, how much money you have, the past decisions you have made, regrets, achievements, wins or losses. "What bike do you ride?" That is the only question that another will ever ask. We do not need to know who you are, or where you come from. This community also has a language. It is the language of hand gestures angled to the side and moving through the air like a plane, depicting that amazing turn that you just rode through. It is the language of cubic centimeters, of tire wear, and oil choices, of suspension settings, of fuel mixtures, and mileage logged. There is a subtle wave, the gesture of universal understanding when passing another rider on the road. I do not know you, I do not see the color of your skin, the features of your face, or your status. I see that you are riding toward me atop a machine and that is more than enough for me to know we are one and the same. It does not matter what you are riding, where you are going, or where you have been, it is just you and your machine that is enough for me. So I give you a small wave, sometimes it is a hand, two fingers, or even just a nod. It is to say, you are my brother, you are my sister, be safe. I do not believe that this gesture, this sense of community exists anywhere on our planet.

Solitude

Escape and solitude are often paired together. We exist in a world surrounded by stimuli and stress, of love and laughter, of happiness and sadness. Moto provides us with the chance to be alone. This idea is calm. It is peace. In this moment your decisions impact you, they impact those immediately around you on the road, and each action you take, whether it is to accelerate, to brake, to shift gears, to move left, to move right, these actions bring reaction. There are few moments in life where we have complete control over our path and actions. Moto is one of them. It is a moment to control yourself, the machine beneath you, and to let go of everything else. In this moment of solitude, there is no choice but to be present. Mindfulness is an idea born from solitude. These moments, each passing second, they are irreplaceable. Solitude springs an overwhelming sense of personal responsibility. The choices you make, in your life, and while you are riding, they are yours and yours alone.

You are moto....

The Frame

Like the bones that make up your precious vessel, the frame of your moto provide the structure needed to carry the weight of your life. Each angle built to withstand the force necessary to provide the strength, the flexibility, and the comfort of the ride. The welds, each carefully constructed to bind the structure of your ride so delicately together.

The Controls

Stop and go. These are your controls, and quite perfectly the things that you can control. The controls provide you the opportunity to tame the machine that lies beneath you and command it to merge with your very being to become an entity of one. From the clutch, which allows you to release the pressure from your main drive, to choose if you will shift up or down to change the interaction with your road ahead. To the throttle, which allows you to set the pace for which you attack the obstacles that lie in your path. And your brakes, the choice you make to slow yourself down, to ease into the places you need to be to perform at your very best.

The Wheels

The balance of life. Of happiness and of sadness is found beneath our machine. They connect us to the road, with a precise level of pressure, to ground us, to keep us safe, to guide as along our path with a center and precision of utmost balance.

The Engine

Our heart, our soul. The engine of a machine, made up of thousands of parts, all interconnected, to bring power, and motion, action and reaction. The precise timing of valves, cranks, pumps, pistons, fuel, fire, air, and oil. It is nothing short of magical science.

The Exhaust

Some of us are loud. Some of us are not. The heat of our lives, the mixture of our decisions and our experiences, must escape somewhere. The exhaust of your bike allows for the reaction of power to be unleashed, it allows for the air to flow through your machine, breathing life to the engine and propelling the past outward for a new experience. Our lives are the same. We intake so much in our daily lives, every moment, every decision we make it gets sucked into our soul, mixes with our experiences, and the leaves us as we make decisions and move in our own direction.

The Line You Leave Behind

Where we go, we leave ourselves. There is nothing that we do, nowhere that we ride where we do not leave the impression of our presence on the road and on those around us. The beauty of our line is that is ever changing. The grains of our life shift as the grains under our machine. We blow through life, forging a path ahead for those that will come after us, and in honor of those that came before. What line will you leave in the ground?

The human spirit is no different than the components of a motorcycle. We are made of the pieces of our experience. Defined in purpose, crafted by a creator for a role. The drive we have inside each of us. Our passion is our fire for learning. Our air the is the opportunity to conquer our dreams. The fire provides the spark for those around us. Each of us has the ability to impact the world in profound ways. When all of these elements are combined, it is magical science.

When I ride the fear of failure, loss, heartache, depression, despair, they fade. The brain doesn't have the ability to fear the unknown in the moments between gear shifts.

This is my story....

I was five years old when I first heard the cackling sound of a two-stroke dirt bike. Englishtown, NJ. The state of Bruce Springsteen, Bon Jovi, the Jersey Shore, and my family. My brother was my shining light, everything that he ever wanted to do .... I did. We had a shed out back that housed his race quad. There it sat, the freedom machine. The chance to escape his world. To feel the moment of a machine, sliding through corners. I idolized him and his ability to be free. Before I was granted the chance to twist my throttle into the sunset of freedom, I had to use the two most efficient engines that I had, my two legs. Donning my Ninja Turtle helmet, I raced from curb jump to curb jump, sliding into turns at blazing speed, slamming the brakes, letting my inner animal wild and free, until mom called me in for dinner. The idea of being in control, while losing control, and really having no control is a concept that I would learn to coexist with for my entire adult life to this point. I would rush home after school each day to dig, shovel and build the best two foot jumps my heart could imagine. I would take wood and blocks and erect the greatest freestyle motocross track known to mankind. I would fly what seemed to be 90 feet in the air when in reality it was probably closer to 9 inches of freedom. There was no fighting then, no money, no debates, no politics. It was the moment that we all seem to seek now in our older age. Freedom.

1989 Yamaha YZ80

I grew up lucky. My family had worked their whole lives, generations had come over from their home countries to give me the chance to swing a leg over an old dirt bike. My mother, a saint on earth, worked her way from an Irish Catholic family in New Jersey to provide her children with a life that she could only dream as a child. My father, the son of a hard working Italian mother and a WWII veteran father who instilled a strong work ethic and a loving spirit. My dad had worked his way from the streets of Jersey City, NJ to the Twin Towers of the financial world. I was a lucky one. My family moved from several smaller houses when I was a child but the better part of my early childhood, I was raised in a large house with a basement full of toys. On my 11th birthday my dream came true. You see I am a weird kid. I didn't like parties, too many friends, or a lot of hustle and bustle. Playing in the basement was my preferred way of life. And so to me, at 11 years old, the chance to be alone atop a dirt bike was the dream of freedom.

It was an average day a few days after my 11th birthday when I came home to my family ushering me outside to our backyard. As I turned the corner, there she was, in all the glory of the world, a white and red stallion of dreams. A 1989 Yamaha YZ80. The # 17 stuck on her side panels from a previous owner. What was her story? What owner had purchased this bike new from the dealer floor? For whom was this amazing piece of Japanese technology? These are the thoughts that raced through my head as even at that young age I fell in love with the story. It was at that moment that I became *The Dirt Bike Kid*, I became Rick from *Winners Take All*. For the uninitiated these are two of the greatest movies ever created to not win an Oscar. In my humble opinion that should have won an Oscar in every category and then created a few new categories. Donning my brothers hot pink JT chest protector and JT racing pants I would race into the yard to tear off laps and drive the neighbors nuts. It is in this bike that I had found my very best friends.

A neighbor well beyond my years who taught me life through a deck of poker cards. A best friend who always made me feel like I was part of a duo that could not be matched. As I zipped around the backyard I felt like the king of the world. The YZ80 was my childhood. The day that this changed was the day that we had to move. Unknown to me my father had lost his job and we were set on a new path. One of uncertainty and one that would take me on a journey through the world of two wheels for many different reasons.

As we settled into our new house, the YZ80 settled into a new story. My time for riding seemed to slip away and so my childhood went to a new family, to form new memories, new laughs, and new moments of glory.

During this time my brother worked at a motorcycle dealer which gave me the chance to attend the motorcycle shows. The ability to throw a leg over, well, more like hop a leg onto the bikes of your dreams at 8 years old was the best day a kid could ask for. The shine of the new plastics, the feel of unworn grips, the signs dangling from the handlebar showing a price that as a kid you had no idea how you were going to be able to afford, but you knew one day you would. The best part of this experience though was spending these moments with my father and my brother.

There was always a bike. Motorcycles are the only thing that I have truly found passion in. Sport interests have come and gone but my love for two wheels has always been present. Trips to the local motorcycle dealer were what we did on a Saturday afternoon with nothing to do. Just the ability to go look, to walk into that building and see all of the potential avenues for riding was exhilarating. One afternoon I came upon the most beautiful sight, a brand new 1998 Yamaha YZ125. I was 13, I had no job, no income, barely enough money saved up for a pair of riding gloves, but I knew that if I could just figure out a way to pay $62 a month that bike could be mine.

1993 Kawasaki KX125

My brother is my moto hero. He raced quads growing up but when his racing career took a turn after a severe injury he traded his quad for a 1993 KX125. This bike is my high school. Over time I asked my brother if it was ok if I rode this bike and more and more this bike became a shared experience for the two of us. I would come home from school, don my now slightly improved gear, a blue MSR pant and shirt set and the matching helmet to go along with it. I would cruise throughout the neighborhood, pretending to be on a test ride so the neighbors didn't immediately complain, and then tear off into the construction area for a quick turn track until dinner. It was again my escape to freedom, a word that I didn't understand the definition, but I knew the feeling. I would go to the local motorcross track and wouldn't jump more than 3 inches off the ground. But when a picture of me ended up in the school yearbook that didn't stop me from signing autographs in everyone's yearbook like I was a national champion.

My bike timeline shifted with my life as I prepared to go off to college. I lost touch with my ability to ride each day. For my high school graduation I took every dollar that I got and I bought:

1998 Kawasaki ZX6R

She was rough beyond compare. Fractured track body work, missing pieces at every turn but she had, potential. She was me at 18 years old. I bought this bike with the intention of turning it into a track day bike. I would come home on the weekends I figured and take my dad and brother to watch me zoom into the history books. None of that happened. I went to college in New York City and this became my escape. I didn't have a bike to ride but rather a city to ride and explore. They are one and the same to me though. The drumming heartbeat of NYC is like the roar of a mighty V-Twin. I spent my days and nights exploring each corner of this magical city. Reeling in its pain and celebrating its wonder. This time of my life was a time of learning, of clear direction, and of self discovery. I learned what I was capable of and certainly what I was not. It was here in the time of the ZX6 that I learned the words anxiety and depression. The rushing feeling of being trapped without breath, with a world unreal, the crushing weight of one's own thoughts, and the doubt that it would truly ever change. I had a relationship end during the ZX6. It was one that grounded me but also distracted me from the truth of my life. We tend to find these in our lives, we call them escapes, we call them distractions, but they are chances to ignore the reality of your time, and hide within the walls of safety. And so, alone in this giant city I rode the laps of this city of dreams. While I did that the ZX6 sat, with its own overwhelming potential as a bike untapped. I did not know its story. Where had it been purchased? For whom was it purchased? Where was that owner now? You see these machines, they aren't much different than we are, and they are a part of own stories. They have a soul, made up of their previous owners or builders. When I look at a bike I see the joy of the first owner as she or he brought it home. I see in that same owner, the pain of the first scratch. I see the despair of those that needed to sell it because life presented them with a more dire situation. In each machine lives lifetimes of experiences. The ZX6R would sit, unloved, in my family garage until I would eventually sell it to a friend who could give it a better life. Like a member of my own family, I find myself checking in from time to time with my friend who still owns this bike and it brings me joy to know its potential has finally been revealed. For me, this bike represents me at that time in my life. I didn't possess the ability to repair this bike just as I didn't have the ability to repair myself. I didn't have the time to dedicate to the understanding of what was wrong inside myself or the ability to fix either one of us.

2009 Ducati Hypermotard

My first job. My first real chance to begin my life. Everything was lined up perfectly. I had it all. A fiancé, a dog, the path to a home. My life was exactly where I wanted to be according to my "plan". And so it was time for my first real bike. As you can see, up until this point, my riding experience had been dirt bikes. I wanted a bike to ride on the street that would maintain the upright riding position that gave me that sense of being a little kid again. I also wanted the statement of success that I believed that I had at that time. And so there was but one choice, the finely crafted heart and soul of an Italian V-Twin. A Ducati Hypermotard. My brother is my moto idol, have I said that yet? I can remember as a kid hearing him say that a Ducati represented the very best of the motorcycle world. His good friend had a yellow Ducati 748, the most beautiful bike ever created along side its bigger sister the 916. Ducati was a dream. A dream for my brother and so as a result, a dream for me. I couldn't afford to outright buy this dream bike so I did what any brilliant young owner does, I signed those finance papers and away I went into the sunset. I bought the best gear I could buy that made me look as much like Valentino Rossi as possible. A full leather track suit. Yup, I was that guy with a brand new Ducati, a brand new Dainese full leather racing suit, and a three mile suburban loop of traffic. I was nowhere near turn three at Mugello but every back road corner felt like it. This bike was symbol that despite the choices along my path, I had made it. This bike brough with it a new marriage, and a new house, and a new child. And so as we do as young parents, it was time to part ways and prepare as best as possible for the arrival of my little monkey. During the time I owned this piece of art I had only amassed a total of 1,200 miles and so she was in pristine condition like the crown jewel of England. It represented so many aspects of my life. Clean, polished, exactly what the outside world deemed to be perfect. And so on the day it was time for her to find a new story , perhaps there was a sign of things to come in my own story. A nice man from not far down the road came by to take buy my life's work. He gently pulled his small pickup truck into the driveway, dropped the tailgate, and attached a wide loading ramp. We signed the papers, exchanged the money, he sat on the bike and put his foot in position. As a heavy blow to my heart was upon us, his foot slipped on the metal grate and slowly my dreams fell into oblivion. The bike dropped, mirror shattered, pieces of Italian craftsmanship spew into the air all around us. Thankfully for all three of us the damage would be repairable but not the impact. I felt for this gentleman, as the greatest fear we all have when purchasing a bike had come true. He did the unthinkable and dropped the bike before he ever got it home. We had a good nervous laugh as we both took a chance to assess the damage. We shared a moment, as we do in our community of family. I helped him to gather the pieces and we stitched together what we could for his ride home. I watched him pull away and into the sunset went the beginning of my adult story.

2012 Yamaha WR250R

The greatest gift I could ever imagine was to be granted the chance to be a father. I always wanted children and my parents provided me with the example of what a loving parent could accomplish. In my daughter I found a love beyond anything bound to this planet. Her dreams are written in the stars and my life has but one purpose, to love her. I hope that her life is packed full of challenges and obstacles. Not something you read about in the first page of the parenting books. But I hope that she is challenged because in her spirit is the ability to conquer anything that she faces. When my daughter entered the world, I found myself, as many parents do, in a new period of self-discovery. With an empty garage and a house full of baby toys I sought out another chance to refuel with a trip back to my childhood. Escape is a theme amongst many riders in our family. I have found that in my own life the twist of the throttle is more powerful than the bottom of the bottle. And so instead of funding the local bar to find a bit of fuel I sought out a bike built for the every rider, a Yamaha WR250R. This is a bike that shines with versatility. A do it all machine that offered the feeling that I searched for as a child. It was dirt bike on the road, how could I not love this bike? The WR250R provided me with the chance to explore in a way that I was unable to do previously. The chance to find a beaten path, to imagine that I was coming around last lap at the LA Coliseum avoiding hay bales like Ricky Johnson and chasing down Jeff Stanton. By firing up that single cylinder and heading to the rural roads I was able to be transported to that place we seek.

The transition from buying the best bike possible to taking apart a bike piece by piece, to learning the intricacies and quicks or each component, was the next step in my moto journey. Moto has taught me lessons that I never thought possible. I have learned that for a truly successful life you must find a person that you can understand how each component of their soul works. Know it, understand it, love each part for the role it plays, and appreciate that complete masterpiece that is their human being. When you find this person to share your life with, examine their inner magic to see what drives them, what fuels them, what breaks them, and what builds them. Love them, give them every drop of passion, fuel and fire, and entrust in them all of your worldly fears. Lean into them and commit to the jump.

2004 Suzuki RM125

I found myself at a place in life where it was time to examine my pieces, and to do that I had to start with a bike. While I had spent my life up to this point loving the look, the sound, the feel of motorcycles, I know wanted to know what magic lay inside these tamely beasts. To this point I didn't quite understand how it all worked. And so came the 2004 Suzuki RM125. As I wanted to take on my first rebuild. I found a specimen with a similar story to my own. The previous owner, a young man in his teenage years, was more advanced in his journey than I as he had sought the answers earlier than I had. He had begun the disassembly process and so I bought a bike in a box, well, in several boxes. This bike gave me the chance to touch every nut and bolt. I repainted the frame, rebuilt the suspension, rebuilt both the full top and bottom end of the engine, laced my own wheels, inserted new tubes, rebuilt the carburetor, donned it with a new exhaust, plastics, and a graphics kit. This bike was surely mine. This experience taught me lessons that I never anticipated and the process of tearing down a soul to rebuild it, well that is a part of life that we will talk about a bit later.

After my rebuild, I was feeling quite good about my abilities as a groundbreaking mechanic and so I did what any other true human would do. I spent the next two years searching online marketplaces for projects that I could control, fix, rebuild, and find a new owner. Looking back now this was my attempt, to control a world that was shaking around me and would prove the toughest test I have ever faced. In the months and years to follow this rebuild I found myself divorced. This time brought uncertainty, a restart of my path, fear, pain, doubt, a lack of faith and trust in myself, and a freedom to begin to rebuild a new soul in myself. Just as I tore down the RM125 to learn each component I had to tear down myself, find my purpose, connect myself to the things that brought me closer to whole, and set out on my new course.

2000 Ducati 748 Mono

And so, in the midst of a divorce, I made the only decision I could gather, I bought yet another bike. This time I took a trip back to my childhood and attempted to regain a sense of self in the memories of freedom. There was only one bike that could accomplish this task. The most beautiful bike ever created, the Ducati 748. This lady was born a screaming Italian yellow but had been repainted in a black and white color scheme at some point during her story. The owner that I bought this Italian classic from did not care well for the bike. I instantly fell in love with the story of this machine and figured while I tried to rebuild myself it would be important to rebuild this bike.

This 748 was raw and struggling to maintain its aging beauty. The previous owner did not put the time and attention required to keep such a beautiful bike where it belonged. Once the glory of this bike has been regained it was like nothing I had experience. It popped, snarled, and roared its way through our journey. One evening while visiting the local town center an older gentlemen stopped me to explain that I needed to find a mechanic as soon as possible because this bike sounded like it was broken. I gently explained to this man that this sound was simply that of the dry clutch spinning its way through the hearts of decades of Italian motorcycle enthusiasts. I spent two years with this fine piece of Italian craftsmanship before it was time to find another home. I have never had a bike punish me for this attempt. One evening while I was showing the bike to a potential owner in the downtown area of our town the bike showed me how it truly felt about this endeavor. Despite having a brand-new battery and solid electrical wiring recently checked, upon arrival of the buyer the bike refused to start. I had ridden the bike to that location not five minutes prior but there was no life to be found. After several futile minutes the potential buyer bid me farewell and good luck and I could not blame this young gentleman for his departure. And so there we sat, the Italian and I. I explained to this lovely bike my reasons for finding it a new home but that appeared to only anger it more. To my left there sat a four story parking garage that presented the only chance I had at a ride home that evening. And so, will a line of cars waiting behind me, I pushed that 748 up to the top of the parking structure and began the pop start process. It took two whole trips up that structure to get it to fire up and begrudgingly take me home. I would eventually diagnose the problem and find this lovely beast a beautiful home. I will always remember that bike as the one that didn't want to get away.

2014 Ducati Streetfighter 848

A new beginning. Enter the Ducati Streetfighter 848. The previous owner was a woman who cared for the bike with the fine hand of an artist. Every maintenance was meticulously noted, every inch of the bike was kept free of even the smallest grain of dirt or grime. As we have seen from earlier exploits of mine I have fascination with the desmodromic driven V-Twin rawness of Italy's greatest export. The 848 comes at a time in my story where I have ridden the waves of highs and lows. I have put my faith in myself and in not knowing what the future may bring.

The Space Between

Up until this point I had been lying to myself. I believed that if I bought things and took risks that I didn't need to take that it would undo the years of making decisions that hid my truth. And it caught up. It was time for a restart. I sold my house and the SF 848 and set myself on a new course. But this space between was quiet. There was no open road. There was no salvation. There was just me, sitting in the middle of the road, staring down the speeding semi-truck that carried all my past decisions. I needed yet again, a why.

1987 Honda VFR 700

The VFR is a story of reflection and rebirth. This bike had been to-taled by a previous owner as decisions were made that nearly cost this bike its life. However, along came someone who saw what was left of these broken pieces and decided to put it back together. This person wasn't me. This wonderful soul saw what was special and unique about this bike and what it could become. They put countless hours rebuild-ing each component of this machine to forge an opportunity for a second chance. And so, with 27,000 miles and 36 years she came into my life. This bike is about second chances. For both of us. It is not the snarling visceral ride of the Ducati's that have come before. However, it shares the beautiful hum of a vertical four-cylinder heart. It is the smoothest and most zen inspiring bike I have ever owned. And perhaps that is the beauty of this reflection. I have lost everything that I thought was key to my happiness. And though, where there is still work to be done, I am finding peace in the search for my truth.

My Why

When I turn my head to see a glimpse of the road behind me it has been a track with a series of turns. And on that track there has existed a gambit of ruts. How do I define a rut? It is a single line, in a single corner, on a single track. Made up of small grains of earth. That line can never be replicated, it changes everyday, with every lap. No rut is truly experienced the same. Just the same, our lives are constantly changing shape. They are made up of the grains of our experiences. And so, I have found that when faced with a rut, we commit to the line, we lean over, farther than we are comfortable with, we trust ourselves, we look through the turn, passed the giant dark hole staring us in the face, and we give it gas. We fire toward the next turn, that next jump, that next challenge. Sometimes, we completely fall on our face. Yet that rut does not consume our entire life. We do not move all of our worldly possessions into that rut and lay there. We can't see the next turn, all we see is that hole and we are afraid how much that next fall may hurt. Then suddenly you realize have been here before and it has been difficult. Yet today, you know what to do. Settle in, remember the feeling of the bike beneath you, lean over, let go of your comfort, turn your head toward the future, and turn the throttle. At the exit of that turn lies the feeling of a perfectly run corner, despite its bumps, and the perfect amount of power and direction for that next challenge. The speed and momentum you carry is no match for any obstacle that may stand in your way. A perfectly run corner can set you up for the ability to fly higher than you thought possible.

The human form was created to move. As children we develop the love for speed, for the feeling of enhancing our ability, to go further, faster, higher, and with more velocity than our body will take us. This is the feeling we seek.

There is no end to my story yet. I am beginning to find peace with the decisions I have made. And while I look back and think of what could have been I am reminded that there is no reverse gear on any bike I have ever owned. They just don't go backward. In fact, if you try to pick up your feet allow your bike to roll backward into the past, after a certain distance, you will fall over. The throttle does not turn in the opposite direction. And there is no rear view mirror. I feel this is my why. I have regrets in my life. That is my truth. I wish I would have made different decisions. But once I swing my leg over a motorcycle, if I am going to survive that ride, there is only one direction I can face. There is only one turn at a time I can look to, and only one horizon I can catch. Our lives are no different. We can look behind us at what was there before. We can understand what lies around us now. But no matter the effort, the road behind us serves only as a guide of where we have been.

As you embark on this journey, to find your own story, to write a path for your own moto future I will make you a promise. You will never be alone. Loneliness is life's greatest mystery. We can live in a city of 9 million people and feel alone. We can walk in a group of 300 and feel alone. We can have friends and family surrounding us and we can feel alone. Until we raise our voice and say hello. This community will provide you with the chance to say hello. You will feel loved, cared for, embraced, and surrounded by a family of souls akin to your own.

And so I ask this of you. Reflect on your own experience. The bikes you have purchased, built, neglected, completed, crashed, sold, handed down, and the ones that have sat strongly with you through your life and are still waiting to greet you in your garage.

Give yourself to this bike, give yourself to this life. Give up all hesitation for pain, for fear. Do not let the negative aspects of life or riding stop you from grabbing a handful of life. You will crash. You will fall. You will fail. This I am certain. When you think the road ahead is smooth, when you have filled your tank with gas, checked your tire pressure, changed your oil, cleaned every inch of your machine and your soul, and perfected your technique... you will slide, you will swerve, you will hit the ground harder than you ever thought possible. If you survive this fall you will be faced with a choice. You can give up. Or you can stand up, and rebuild. Your body, your relationships, your goals, your focus, your life, and your bike. How? You do this piece by piece. You take a look around. You check your body and take note of what hurts so you can tend to it at a later time. You will be bruised and your bike will be missing pieces. If you are lucky, there will be those in your life that love you, that will be there to help you find the pieces and pick them back up again. So start with the small pieces as they will let you know where the greater damage may be. Mend those pieces that are broken and in this process you may find that there are some that need to be replaced. However, I believe you will find that the pieces that you fear are lost, can often be saved. With extra care, attention, love, and patience you can forge these pieces into something stronger than they were before. It will take time, it will take more pain, sweat, tears, and often blood. In these moments you will find a window into life's greatest reward. To examine each piece of ourselves. To know exactly what each part does. To know the strength and weakness of each component of our soul. Piece by piece your bike will come back together. One bolt, one wire, one turn of the wrench at a time. Then one day, when you least expect it, you will step back and realize you, and your bike are ready to ride again. There is no guarantee that you won't crash again. No guarantee that you will not feel pain, and loss once again. No guarantee that you won't have to pick up the pieces, again. But when you choose to turn your key, to swing a leg over your seat, to settle back into the way of life you know well and you allow yourself to escape your fears, find your freedom, embrace your community, find peace in your solitude, seek your adventure, then along your path, you will find your why.

This... is Why we Moto.

WHY MOTO